COLE'S COOKING COMPANION

W9-CKA-523

SIZZLE
BARBECUING & GRILLING

COLE GROUP

Both U.S. and metric units are provided for all recipes in this book. Ingredients are listed with U.S. units on the left and metric units on the right. The metric quantities have been rounded for ease of use; as a result, in some recipes there may be a slight difference (approximately ½ ounce or 15 grams) between the portion sizes for the two types of measurements.

Printed in Hong Kong

Cole Group, Inc.
1330 N. Dutton Ave., Suite 103
Santa Rosa, CA 95401
(800) 959-2717   (707) 526-2682   Fax (707) 526-2687

Cole Group and Cole's Cooking Companion are trademarks of CHI/Cole Holdings, Inc.

G	F	E	D	C	B	A
1	0	9	8	7	6	5

ISBN 1-56426-801-2

Library of Congress Catalog Card Number in process

Distributed to the book trade by Publishers Group West

Cole books are available for quantity purchases for sales promotions, premiums, fund-raising, or educational use. For more information on *Sizzle: Barbecuing & Grilling* or other Cole's Cooking Companion books, please write or call the publisher.

CONTENTS

Getting Started   5
    Barbecuing Versus Grilling   6
    Cooking Methods   6
    Grills   6
      Preparing the Grill   7
    Fuels and Firestarters   8
    How Much Fire?   10
      Safety Tips   11

From Grill to Table   13
    Marvelous Marinades   14
    Sauces for Barbecue   18
    Beef   22
      When Is Meat Done?   27
    Pork   34
      Microwave-Boosted Barbecue   43
    Lamb   44
    Poultry   50
      Herbal Skewers   53
      When Is Poultry Done?   55
      Flavoring the Fire   57
      Safety Tips for Fresh Poultry   61
    Seafood   62
      Grilling Times for Fish   65
      Timing Grilled Skewers   66
      Tips for Grilling Fish   71
    Vegetables   76
      Preparing Eggplant for the Grill   79
      Kids Cooking at the Grill   86
    Fruit   88
      Tips for Grilling Fruit   91

Index   95

GETTING STARTED

*T*he original method of heating food—over an open flame—has evolved into two broad categories, each with its own techniques. Mastering the art of barbecuing and grilling is a matter of understanding basic outdoor cooking methods and techniques, having the right equipment for the job, and choosing good-quality ingredients for the recipes you prepare. The information that follows is designed to start you on your way to experiencing the thrill of the grill.

Barbecuing versus Grilling

Barbecuing produces a distinctive smoky aroma and flavor, the result of a relatively cool (225°F or 110°C) wood or charcoal fire, slow cooking, and a tangy sauce (there are innumerable styles) that permeates the food as it cooks. *Grilling* also imparts a smoky quality. Grilled foods are prepared from fresh ingredients cooked quickly over a hot fire (approximately 500°F or 260°C or more).

Cooking Methods

All the recipes in this book specify which cooking method—direct heat or indirect heat—to use, whether the food is to be barbecued or grilled. The method you use depends on the type of food and the results you're after.

The *direct-heat method*—cooking directly over the heat source—sears the food, seals in juices, and produces a characteristic "grilled" appearance. The *indirect-heat method*—slow-cooking over an obstructed heat source—often involves placing a drip pan beneath the food. Sometimes it is filled with water or other liquids to help keep food moist as it cooks.

Grills

Having the right equipment for the job is essential for successful barbecuing and grilling. If you're thinking about purchasing a new grill or accessories, be guided by your budget, the space you have available, and how frequently you cook outdoors. Here's an overview of grill types:

Conventional Grills

These popular grills run the gamut from classic backyard built-ins of brick or stone to go-anywhere portables that take up no more space than a stack of dinner plates.

Covered grills with removable or hinged lids offer economy, portability, and versatility, since they can be used uncovered or covered. *Kettle grills* are rounded versions of covered grills. Most are designed for cooking with the lid closed, which helps prevent flare-ups. If the fire is hot enough, most of these grills also can be used uncovered. ***Open grills*** include braziers, hibachis, and other lidless grills. They are best for cooking foods that don't cause flare-ups, such as fish and lean meats.

GAS AND ELECTRIC GRILLS

The convenience of having a fire ready at the touch of a button can make gas and electric grills a worthwhile investment for many people. And, since these grills produce little smoke, they are popular in localities with anti-pollution ordinances. The capabilities and cost of these grills range from modest tabletop models to top-of-the-line designs with high-tech ignition and heat control systems rivaling those in indoor ranges.

PREPARING THE GRILL

Before you begin, map out the grilling area with an eye to what you'll be cooking. Plan to have some areas of the grill surface with no coals under them. You can move food that is already done to the cooler areas to keep warm while the rest of the food cooks.

- *Start clean. Develop the habit of always cleaning the grill with a grill brush as it heats, before you oil the grill and add the food. Or you can clean the grill immediately after removing the cooked food. Either way takes only a few minutes, since a hot grill is easy to scrape clean, and the fire burns off any lingering debris. Avoid harsh detergents or cleansers, which can ruin the seasoned surface.*

- *Have all your tools— especially tongs, fire-resistant mitts, and a filled spray bottle—handy before you light the fire.*

- *Lightly oil the grill after it has heated 4–5 minutes to keep the cooking surface seasoned and prevent sticking. Moisten a wad of paper toweling with cooking oil and use tongs to wipe the oil across the rack.*

- *Have extra charcoal on hand in case the fire cools before the food is done.*

Gas grills use either liquid propane gas (LP) or natural gas. Most have lava rocks (see photo above), ceramic briquettes, porcelain-coated metal bars, or aluminum plates in the bottom of the grill to evaporate drippings falling from the food above. Heat circulation and temperature control are typically strong points of gas grills. *Electric grills* usually work on the same principle as an oven broiler, only the heating element is beneath the cooking area rather than above it. Easy to use and regulate, they offer many of the same advantages as gas grills.

FUELS AND FIRESTARTERS

The proliferation of different varieties of fuel products can seem confusing, but just remember that virtually all types of fuel work well in the right situation. Experience will help you judge what works best for you.

BRIQUETTES

The fuel of choice for more than 50% of consumers, most briquettes are made from scrap wood, with additives and fillers for consistent burning. Before placing food over briquettes, wait until they are coated with a thin layer of gray ash.

HARDWOOD CHARCOALS

Made from woods such as apple, cherry, hickory, maple, mesquite, and oak, without additives or fillers, hardwood (lump) charcoals lend a pleasant smoky flavor. Mesquite charcoal burns hotter than other hardwoods, and the coals can be re-used several times; however, mesquite tends to pop burning embers into the air, so use it with caution.

CHUNKS, CHIPS, AND SAWDUST

Ash, alder, apple, cherry, grapevine, hickory, maple, mesquite, oak, olive, and other varieties of aromatic chunks, chips, and sawdust all contribute distinctive character to grilled foods. Always be sure that hardwood used for the grill has aged at least one year. Never use pine or other softwoods; the resins produce an unpleasant aftertaste. Also avoid scrap wood and pressure-treated lumber (the type used in outdoor construction), which releases toxic chemicals while burning.

Aromatic woods are best used with covered grills, which allow the smoke they produce to be contained so it can permeate the food. Chunks or chips should be soaked in water before being distributed evenly over the hot coals. For sawdust, place a handful in an old metal pie tin and place it directly atop the hot coals, which will cause it to smolder. For best results, follow manufacturer's directions for the particular type of grill and fuel you are using.

FIRESTARTERS

After you light briquettes or charcoal, allow 30–45 minutes for the fire to burn down before you add the food. Be sure to follow the Safety Tips (see page 11).

Kindling Crumple newspaper into wads or "logs" and add a handful of dry kindling on top. Place five or six briquettes on top of the kindling and light the newspaper. Once the briquettes light, add more on top until you have a fire of the desired size.

Chemical Lighters Chemical starters (fluid, blocks, or cubes) are convenient, although some release pollutants that can taint the flavor of grilled foods.

Follow all safety procedures listed on the package or container. Never squirt fluid lighter directly onto a burning fire; the flame can travel back up the stream and burn your hands and arms, or even ignite the container! Never use gasoline, naphtha, paint thinner, or kerosene as firestarters—they are too flammable.

Electric Starters These are convenient (assuming you have an AC outlet nearby), safe (assuming you follow the manufacturer's recommendations), and more environmentally friendly than chemical starters.

Charcoal Chimneys These simple metal cylinders are inexpensive and easy to use, producing smoldering briquettes in about 10 minutes. A charcoal chimney is also handy for replenishing your fire with fresh coals. Simply set the chimney on an old pie pan on a concrete surface, fill it with briquettes, and light the newspaper kindling in the bottom. When the briquettes are ready, add them to your existing fire.

HOW MUCH FIRE?

Bigger's not always better when it comes to cooking fires. To determine what size fire you need, envision the cooking surface the food requires. Spread the briquettes out in a single layer to cover an area slightly larger than needed. Add half again as much charcoal, and you should have enough for an hour's worth of cooking. Usually 30–40 briquettes are sufficient to cook food for four people. For slow cooking using the indirect-heat method (see page 6), use about 25 briquettes on each side of the grill. Plan on adding 8–10 briquettes to each side for every hour of additional cooking time.

IS THE FIRE READY?

Allow between 30–45 minutes after lighting for a charcoal fire to become ready for cooking. The coals should be covered with a light ash and no longer flaming. To judge when a fire is ready for cooking, hold your hand flat over the fire at grill height.

- If the fire is too intense for you to hold your hand over it for even a second, let the coals burn down a bit more.

- If the fire is very hot (desirable for the direct-heat method of cooking), you should be able to hold your hand over it for about 2 seconds.

- If the fire is hot or medium-hot (desirable for the indirect-heat method), you can hold your hand above it for 3–4 seconds.

- If you can hold your hand over the fire for longer than 3–4 seconds, the fire has died down too much and needs replenishing with fresh coals (see Charcoal Chimneys on page 10).

SAFETY TIPS

- *Do not use grills in high winds or within 6 feet of combustible materials.*

- *Check to see that grill is level and well-situated before you light the fire. Never attempt to reposition a hot grill.*

- *Do not add lighter fluid to hot or even warm coals. Keep lighter fluid capped and stored a safe distance from the fire.*

- *Be careful where you set hot grill lids, skewers, and grillware when you remove them from the grill.*

- *After grilling, be sure that all "live" coals have completely burned out before removing excess ashes and used briquettes.*

- *Never leave children or pets unattended anywhere near a hot grill.*

FROM GRILL TO TABLE

*F*or sheer sensory enjoyment, nothing
surpasses the aroma, visual excitement,
and flavor of foods hot off the grill.
In this section you'll find more than
50 recipes for marinades and sauces,
beef, pork, lamb, poultry, fish and
shellfish, vegetables and
vegetarian dishes, and desserts.

MARVELOUS MARINADES

Marinades are marvelous in the way they can tenderize, preserve moisture, and enhance the flavor of many grilled meats, fish, vegetables, and even fruit.

Foods can marinate for at least one hour, overnight, or even longer, depending upon the desired intensity of flavor and the time available. Foods marinating for an hour or less can be left out at room temperature; otherwise marinating should take place in the refrigerator. Allow to warm to room temperature (about 30 minutes) before grilling. Drain off marinade and blot food to remove excess liquid.

Wet Marinades

A wet marinade, a liquid in which food is steeped, is usually made with oil, seasoning, and an acid such as lemon juice, vinegar, or wine. A liquid marinade can be mixed in a blender or by hand. Marinate in a covered non-aluminum container that holds the food snugly in a single layer. Leftover marinade can be refrigerated in a covered jar for several weeks.

Teriyaki Marinade

For beef, chicken, or fish.

½ cup	soy sauce	125 ml
3 tbl	sugar	3 tbl
½ tsp	ground ginger	½ tsp
1 clove	garlic, minced	1 clove
2 tbl	dry sherry	2 tbl

Makes about ¾ cup (175 ml).

Mustard and Herb Marinade

For lamb or chicken.

⅓ cup	vegetable oil	85 ml
¼ cup	dry white wine	60 ml
1 tbl each	red wine vinegar and lemon juice	1 tbl each
1 clove	garlic, minced	1 clove
1½ tbl	Dijon mustard	1½ tbl
¼ tsp each	salt and sugar	¼ tsp each
⅛ tsp each	dried thyme, oregano, summer savory, and tarragon	⅛ tsp each
dash	white pepper	dash

Makes about 1 cup (250 ml).

Dry Spice Rubs

A dry marinade, a paste that is massaged into the food, is a blend of spices and dried or fresh herbs. Prepare dry spice rubs by combining all ingredients and mixing well.

Rinse and blot all food before marinating. Lightly oil all surfaces, then massage spice rub into food, using from 1–2 tablespoons per pound of food. Let stand for one hour at room temperature.

Spice Rub for Meat

1 tsp	garlic powder	1 tsp
1 tsp	fennel seed, crushed	1 tsp
½ tsp	thyme	½ tsp
2 tsp	freshly ground black pepper	2 tsp
½ tsp	cayenne pepper	½ tsp
1 tbl	paprika	1 tbl
½ tsp	oregano	½ tsp
½ tsp	salt	½ tsp

Makes 3 tablespoons.

Spice Rub for Poultry

1 tsp	garlic powder	1 tsp
2 tsp	tarragon	2 tsp
½ tsp	sage	½ tsp
1 tsp	marjoram	1 tsp
½ tsp	thyme	½ tsp
2 tsp	freshly ground black pepper	2 tsp
½ tsp	cayenne pepper	½ tsp
1 tbl	paprika	1 tbl
½ tsp	salt	½ tsp

Makes 3 tablespoons.

Spice Rub for Fish

2 tsp	grated lemon rind	2 tsp
1 tsp	garlic powder	1 tsp
1 tsp	tarragon	1 tsp
1 tsp	basil	1 tsp
2 tsp	freshly ground black pepper	2 tsp
½ tsp	cayenne pepper	½ tsp
1 tbl	paprika	1 tbl
½ tsp	salt	½ tsp

Makes about 4 tablespoons.

SAUCES FOR BARBECUE

Barbecue refers both to a style of cooking as well as the sauce used. Sauces for barbecued food reflect regional influences and individual taste. Experiment with the following basic recipes, adding cayenne pepper, jalapeños, habañeros, serranos, or hot-pepper sauce for extra heat or other ingredients to suit your taste. Most sauces will keep in a covered jar for up to a week refrigerated and freeze well for several months.

Georgia Sauce

This mild-tasting easy-to-prepare sauce works equally well with beef, pork, chicken (see page 51), and fish.

1½ cups	tomato purée, canned	350 ml
1 cup	cider vinegar	250 ml
½ cup	oil	125 ml
⅓ cup	Worcestershire sauce	85 ml
½ cup	firmly packed dark brown sugar	125 ml
¼ cup	molasses	60 ml
3 tbl	mustard	3 tbl
2 tsp	minced garlic	2 tsp
¼ cup	lemon juice	60 ml

In a large non-aluminum saucepan, combine all ingredients. Simmer for 15 minutes. Stir often to prevent sauce from burning. Allow sauce to rest for at least 1 hour after cooking to allow flavors to meld, then store in covered container in refrigerator.

Makes 3 cups (700 ml).

North Carolina Sauce

North Carolina barbecue emphasizes the simplicity of slowly roasted meat accented with vinegar—no tomato sauce here. Traditional cooks serve plain cider vinegar alongside the barbecue sauce at the table.

1 cup	cider vinegar	250 ml
2 tbl	crushed red pepper	2 tbl
1 tsp	hot-pepper sauce	1 tsp

Place all ingredients in a small glass container. Cover and shake well to combine, then store in refrigerator.

Makes 1 cup (250 ml).

Texas Sauce

Rich, highly flavored, and perfumed with chile powder, this sauce is excellent for beef, pork, and chicken, but it will overpower fish.

½ cup	butter	125 ml
1 cup	finely chopped onion	250 ml
1 cup	finely chopped celery	250 ml
2 tsp	minced garlic	2 tsp
1 cup	tomato purée, canned	250 ml
½ cup	cider vinegar	125 ml
½ cup	firmly packed dark brown sugar	125 ml
1 cup	beef stock	250 ml
¼ cup	Worcestershire sauce	60 ml
2	bay leaves	2
2 tsp	freshly ground black pepper	2 tsp
2 tsp	cayenne pepper	2 tsp
1 tsp	ground cumin	1 tsp
2 tsp	chile powder	2 tsp
to taste	salt	to taste

In a large non-aluminum saucepan, melt butter and sauté onion, celery, and garlic until soft (about 10 minutes). Add remaining ingredients and simmer for about 30 minutes. Stir frequently so that sauce doesn't burn. Allow sauce to rest for at least 1 hour, then store covered in refrigerator.

Makes 4 cups (900 ml).

Kansas City Sauce

The liquid smoke flavoring re-creates the flavor of meat slowly smoked in the famous Kansas City barbecue pits. If you like spicy barbecue, add 1–2 tablespoons ground cayenne pepper. This thick, sweet sauce works well with beef, pork, or chicken; its flavor is too strong for fish.

½ cup	oil	125 ml
1	onion, finely chopped	1
½	green bell pepper, finely chopped	½
2 tsp	minced garlic	2 tsp
16 oz	catsup	450 g
½ cup	molasses	125 ml
2 tsp	hot pepper sauce	2 tsp
¼ cup	yellow mustard	60 ml
2 tbl	cider vinegar	2 tbl
½ cup	firmly packed dark brown sugar	125 ml
4 tbl	Worcestershire sauce	4 tbl
1 tsp	liquid smoke flavor	1 tsp
¼ cup	lemon juice	60 ml

Heat oil in a large non-aluminum saucepan, then sauté onion, green pepper, and garlic until soft (about 10 minutes). Add the remaining ingredients and continue to simmer slowly for 20–30 minutes. Stir frequently to prevent sauce from burning. Let rest for at least 1 hour after cooking to allow the flavors to meld.

Makes 4 cups (900 ml).

BEEF

The tenderness of a cut of beef determines the method of cooking to use. Tender cuts from the loin—New York strip, T-bone, porterhouse, club, top-sirloin, and filet mignon—or from the prime rib—variously called rib-eye or delmonico—can all be grilled over direct heat. These all are tender enough to cook without a marinade, but a marinade gives extra flavor. Cuts from the chuck, rib, shank, flank, or leg need a tenderizing marinade prior to direct-heat cooking or else should be cooked over indirect heat.

GRILLED STEAK IN HERB CRUST

The spice rub blackens during grilling, forming a delicious, pungent herb crust. Top-sirloin steak is featured here, but you can easily substitute New York strip, filet mignon, or T-bone.

10–12 oz each	4 top-sirloin steaks	285–350 g each
2–3 tbl	olive oil	2–3 tbl
3 tbl	Spice Rub for Meat (see page 16)	3 tbl
as needed	oil, for grill	as needed
4 tbl	unsalted butter	4 tbl

1. Lightly coat steaks with olive oil, then massage meat with spice rub until well coated. Cover and let rest for at least 1 hour at room temperature to allow spices to imbue meat with flavor.

2. Prepare fire for direct-heat method (see page 6). If using a gas grill, use hardwood sawdust for a smoky flavor. If using charcoal, add presoaked hardwood chunks.

3. When fire is very hot, place steaks on oiled grill and cook for 3–5 minutes on each side (depending on thickness of steak and the degree of doneness desired; see page 27). Keep the lid closed during cooking. Baste the steaks once on each side with butter. Remove from fire and serve immediately.

Serves 4.

SESAME BEEF RIBS

Start this dish the day before serving it by marinating the ribs overnight. Most of the flavoring is accomplished in the marinating, which tenderizes the meat and imbues it with hints of sesame and the fragrance of garlic. Use a mesquite fire to round out the flavors.

2	green onions, finely chopped	2
1 tsp	minced garlic	1 tsp
¼ cup	soy sauce	60 ml
¼ cup	sesame oil	60 ml
¼ cup	rice vinegar	60 ml
2 tsp	sesame seed	2 tsp
2 tbl	sugar	2 tbl
1 tsp	dry mustard	1 tsp
1 tsp	freshly ground black pepper	1 tsp
4 lb	trimmed beef ribs	1.8 kg

1. Prepare marinade by combining all ingredients except ribs. Score ribs almost to the bone every ½ inch (1.25 cm). Rub in marinade, cover, and refrigerate 8–12 hours. Turn ribs several times to marinate evenly.

2. Prepare fire for direct-heat method (see page 6). Remove ribs from marinade and reserve marinade. Allow ribs to come to room temperature. Place ribs on grill over hot fire and close lid. Turn ribs several times during cooking and baste with reserved marinade. Ribs are done when they have a crispy exterior and are rare and tender at the bone (about 15 minutes). Serve immediately.

Serves 4.

SOUTHWESTERN STEAK RANCHERO

Serve with rice, a green salad, tortillas, and salsa.

2 tbl	oil	2 tbl
1	onion, cut into thin wedges	1
2 cloves	garlic, minced	2 cloves
5	mild green chiles, roasted, peeled, and cut into strips	5
2	tomatoes, cut into thin wedges	2
2 tbl	chopped cilantro (coriander leaves)	2 tbl
2–3 lb	steak (top-sirloin or rib-eye)	.9–1.4 kg

1. Heat the oil in a skillet and sauté onion and garlic until soft. Add chiles and tomatoes and sauté briefly until soft. Stir in cilantro and keep warm.

2. Prepare fire for direct-heat method (see page 6). When fire is very hot, grill the steaks to individual preference and serve topped with the sautéed chile-tomato mixture.

Serves 6 to 8.

WHEN IS MEAT DONE?

Many master chefs use this hand test rather than a meat thermometer to check meat for doneness.

1. Let one hand dangle freely, relaxing it completely. With the forefinger of your other hand, touch the meaty area between your thumb and forefinger. This is what a piece of rare meat should feel like.

2. Now make a loose fist with your hand. Touch the same place again. This is what a piece of meat cooked to medium should feel like.

3. Now tightly clench your fist. Touch the same place again. This is what a well-done piece of meat should feel like.

BOURBON BEEF TENDERLOIN

Buy a whole tenderloin and have the butcher remove the "silver" (the shiny connective tissue that covers the top). What is left is an absolutely buttery-tender piece of meat. A charcoal or gas grill with a lid works equally well for this dish.

1 cup	bourbon	250 ml
1 cup	brown sugar	250 ml
⅔ cup	soy sauce	150 ml
1 bunch	cilantro (coriander leaves), chopped	1 bunch
½ cup	fresh lemon juice	125 ml
1 tbl	Worcestershire sauce	1 tbl
2 cups	water	500 ml
1 tsp	dried thyme	1 tsp
4½–5 lb	beef tenderloin	2–2.3 kg
as needed	oil, for grill	as needed

1. Prepare marinade by combining all ingredients except beef and oil.

2. Be sure tenderloin is completely trimmed of any fat and connective tissue. Fold the tail end of the beef back onto itself so that the fillet is of uniform thickness. Pour marinade over meat, cover, and refrigerate 8–12 hours. Turn the fillet over several times during that time.

3. Prepare fire for direct-heat method (see page 6). When fire is ready, place meat on oiled grill, reserving marinade. Cook over high heat with lid closed, turning fillet often. Occasionally baste with marinade. Fillet is cooked rare in about 30 minutes, or when a meat thermometer registers 115°F (46°C). When desired doneness is obtained (see page 27), remove from fire and cover with foil to keep warm. Let rest for 10 minutes so that juices stay in meat. Slice against the grain and serve immediately.

Serves 8 to 10.

Santa Maria Barbecue

The Santa Maria Valley of California's central coast has a barbecue tradition going back to the early Spanish rancheros. Fresh salsa and barbecued beans are traditional accompaniments.

1 recipe	Salsa Cruda (see page 31)	1 recipe
3 lb	sirloin steak or small roast	1.4 kg
1 tsp each	salt and garlic salt	1 tsp each
½ tsp	freshly ground black pepper	½ tsp

1. Prepare Salsa Cruda.

2. Trim meat of excess fat and tough membranes. If using a sirloin tip roast, remove strings and butterfly (cut across grain almost through, then open like a book). Overall thickness should be 2½–3 inches (6.25–7.5 cm). Combine salt, garlic salt, and pepper and rub generously over meat. Set aside to season for up to 2 hours at room temperature, or longer in the refrigerator.

3. One and a half hours before serving time, prepare charcoal fire for direct-heat method (see page 6). When most of the charcoal is burning, add small chunks of oak. Sear meat over hottest part of fire, then move it to a slightly cooler area and cook to taste. Total cooking time depends on size of meat, heat of fire, and type of grill (open or covered); thinner cuts over a hot fire may be cooked to medium-rare in 8–10 minutes per side, but with a slower fire or a larger piece of meat, allow 15–20 minutes per side.

4. Carve thin slices of meat on a cutting board with grooves to catch juices. Transfer slices to a warm platter and moisten with juices. Garnish with salsa; serve immediately.

Serves 6.

Salsa Cruda

For a milder version, substitute 4 fresh mild, long green chiles for the jalapeños or serranos.

1 lb (2 cups)	fresh ripe tomatoes, seeded and cut into ¼-inch (.6 cm) dice	450 g (500 ml)
⅓ cup	finely minced sweet red onion	85 ml
4	fresh jalapeño or serrano chiles, trimmed, seeded, and minced finely	4
¼ cup	minced cilantro (coriander leaves)	60 ml
1 clove	garlic, minced finely	1 clove
2 tbl	lime juice	2 tbl
to taste	salt and freshly ground black pepper	to taste

Combine all ingredients in a small bowl. Taste and correct seasoning if needed. Let stand at room temperature about 30 minutes. Serve the same day, or tightly cover and refrigerate for up to 2 days.

Makes about 3 cups (700 ml).

BEIJING BARBECUE

This version of grill-your-own Mongolian barbecue is popular in Beijing. Diners sitting around a tabletop grill cook their own portions to taste, and eat them sandwich-style, in Chinese buns or mandarin pancakes. You can use any size grill, but see Caution (below).

1–1½ lb	boneless tender beef	450–680g
4–6	eggs (1 per person)	4–6
12	green onions, trimmed	12
	and cut into 2-inch (5 cm) lengths	
as needed	soy sauce, for dipping	as needed
	minced ginger, for dipping	
	minced garlic, for dipping	
	chile oil (bottled), for dipping	
	hot mustard sauce (bottled), for dipping	
	rice vinegar, for dipping	
	Hoisin sauce (bottled), for dipping	

1. Prepare fire for direct-heat method (see page 6). Slice beef thinly across grain into 1- by 3-inch (2.5- by 7.5-cm) pieces. (Partially frozen meat is easier to slice thinly.) Arrange on a serving dish with green onions in center.

2. Set a bowl with a beaten egg at each place, and another for dipping sauce. Pass sauces and condiments for each diner to mix a dipping sauce to taste. Each diner grills meat slices and green onions until done to taste, turning and retrieving with chopsticks. (Allow 15 seconds–1 minute per side, according to taste and heat of fire.) As soon as a slice is cooked, dip immediately and briefly into egg (to help bind sauce) and then into dipping sauce.

Serves 4 to 6.

Caution *Never use tabletop grills on glass or laminated surfaces or near any combustible material. Never grill indoors unless the grill has been specifically designed for indoor use.*

PORK

Tender, sweet pork accepts marinades beautifully and stays moist during cooking. Most cuts of pork can be cooked over direct heat, except for large roasts and heavily marinated cuts, which may cause flare-ups. Use fresh pork for grilling—the cell walls in frozen meat break down during freezing, causing significant water loss and dry, tasteless meat when cooked. Pork should be cooked to well-done, about 145°F (63°C), but not dried out, since it can be ruined by overcooking.

OLD-FASHIONED BARBECUED PORK RIBS

Cooking a slab of ribs whole keeps the meat juicy, and the tomato-based Texas-style barbecue sauce adds flavor. Try experimenting with different varieties of hardwood chips or chunks (see page 9).

2 cups	Texas Sauce (see page 20)	500 ml
3–4 lb	1 slab pork spareribs	1.4–1.8 kg

1. Prepare Texas Sauce.

2. Prepare fire for indirect-heat method (see page 6). Allow coals to cool to a moderate temperature (see page 11). Add pre-soaked wood chips or chunks to coals. When fire is ready, place ribs directly over coals to lightly brown on both sides (3–4 minutes per side). Move ribs over drip pan and close lid. Close vents as necessary to achieve a constant temperature of 225°F (110°C). If fire is still too hot, remove ribs until temperature drops.

3. Place half the barbecue sauce in a saucepan and heat for later use as a condiment; use the other half for basting. When ribs are halfway done (in about 30 minutes) lay a piece of heavy-duty foil under them. Use a fork to pierce foil 10 times, distributing the pokes evenly so that smoke continues to penetrate ribs. Baste with barbecue sauce on top side. Close lid. In 5 minutes baste top again and flip ribs over; now baste the other side. Continue this process of basting and flipping until ribs pull apart easily with your fingers (after about 1 hour total cooking time).

4. Remove ribs from fire and cut between bones with a knife. Serve immediately with reserved hot barbecue sauce.

Serves 2 or 3.

THAI BARBECUED RIBS

This rib recipe shows off the subtler, less fiery side of Thai cuisine. Fish sauce is available in the Asian-food section of most supermarkets.

½ cup	fish sauce	125 ml
¼ cup	sugar	60 ml
2 tsp	salt	2 tsp
1 tbl	freshly ground black pepper	1 tbl
2 tbl	minced garlic	2 tbl
1 tbl	chopped cilantro (coriander leaves)	1 tbl
½ cup	water	125 ml
6–7 lb total	2 slabs pork spareribs	2.8–3.2 kg total

Thai Dipping Sauce

⅔ cup	sugar	150 ml
½ cup	distilled vinegar	125 ml
2 tsp	salt	2 tsp
2 tbl	minced garlic	2 tbl
1	red bell pepper, finely grated	1

1. In a large bowl, combine fish sauce, sugar, salt, pepper, garlic, cilantro, and water. Massage marinade into meat. Cover and refrigerate for 8–12 hours.

2. To prepare sauce, in a small saucepan combine sugar, vinegar, salt, and garlic. Bring to a boil, reduce heat, and simmer until thick (about 5 minutes). Add red pepper to sauce right before serving.

3. Prepare fire for direct-heat method (see page 6). Remove meat from marinade, wipe off excess marinade, and reserve marinade in bowl. Place ribs on grill and brown on both sides (about 5 minutes per side). Baste ribs and close lid. Baste and turn ribs every 10 minutes until done, about 45 minutes total cooking time. Slice between bones and serve with sauce.

Serves 6 to 8.

SICILIAN SPIEDINI

These savory "spiedini" (skewers) combine prosciutto-wrapped pork, bread cubes, and sage, grilled to fragrant perfection and then basted with anchovy-flavored butter.

½ lb	prosciutto, sliced paper thin and cut into 2-inch (5 cm) squares	225 g
2 lb	pork tenderloin, cut in ½-inch (1.25 cm) cubes	900 g
24	skewers	24
48	day old French or Italian bread, in ½-inch (1.25 cm) cubes	48
24	fresh sage leaves	24
as needed	olive oil	as needed

Anchovy Butter

1 cup	unsalted butter	250 ml
3 oz	anchovy fillets, drained and minced	85 g
to taste	lemon juice	to taste

1. Wrap prosciutto around pork cubes. Using small skewers, thread each skewer with a bread cube, a cube of pork, a sage leaf, and a second bread cube. Drizzle olive oil over all and refrigerate overnight.

2. To prepare anchovy butter, in a large skillet, melt butter. Add anchovies; mash to a paste with the back of a wooden spoon. Add lemon juice to taste.

3. Prepare charcoal fire for direct-heat method (see page 6). Grill skewers 9–12 minutes, basting with Anchovy Butter every 2–3 minutes. When pork is fully cooked but not dry, brush again with Anchovy Butter and serve immediately.

Makes 24 cocktail skewers.

PORK CHOPS DIJON

Thick, juicy pork chops with a tart mustard coating are perfect for an end-of-summer grill when the nights begin to grow cool.

3 tbl	Dijon mustard	3 tbl
4	loin pork chops, ¾ inch (1.9 cm) thick	4
1 tsp	dried thyme, crushed	1 tsp
to taste	salt and pepper	to taste

1. Prepare charcoal fire for direct-heat method (see page 6). Spread half the mustard evenly over chops; sprinkle with half the thyme.

2. When fire is ready, grill 6 inches (15 cm) from heat source 10–12 minutes. Turn chops, spread with remaining mustard. Sprinkle with remaining thyme, salt, and pepper to taste.

3. Grill second side until nicely browned (10–12 minutes). Juices should run clear when chop is pierced with a fork at thickest point.

Serves 4.

PORK ADOBO

Adobo is a spicy, chile-vinegar paste in which pork is marinated and then barbecued.

5	dried ancho chiles	5
3	dried California chiles	3
4	cloves garlic, minced	4
1 tsp	dried oregano	1 tsp
½ tsp	ground cumin	½ tsp
¼ tsp	ground cloves	¼ tsp
1 tbl	salt	1 tbl
½ cup	wine vinegar	125 ml
4 lb	pork steaks	1.8 kg
as needed	salsa verde (bottled), for garnish	as needed

1. Remove the stems and seeds from the chiles and discard. Place chiles in a saucepan and add water just to cover. Bring to a boil, reduce heat, and simmer for 5 minutes. Set aside to steep for 30 minutes. Drain the chiles.

2. Place chiles and remaining ingredients except meat and salsa into a blender or food processor and blend briefly to a textured purée. Spread the chile purée over the meat, covering both sides. Rub it in well and cook immediately, or, for maximum flavor, cover with waxed paper and allow to season in the refrigerator for 1–3 days.

3. Prepare fire for direct-heat method (see page 6). Grill steaks to individual preference, applying additional marinade, if desired. Garnish with salsa verde.

Serves 8 to 10.

Caution *The hotter varieties of fresh chiles can burn the skin. If you are going to handle many chiles or if you have tender skin, wear rubber gloves. When handling chiles, keep your hands away from your face, especially your eyes. When finished, wash your hands (or rubber gloves) thoroughly with soap and water.*

CHINESE BARBECUED PORK LOIN

Bathing the pork in a marinade adds to the succulent richness of this Asian specialty. The tenderloins cook very quickly.

½ cup	soy sauce	125 ml
¼ cup	sesame oil	60 ml
¼ cup	rice vinegar	60 ml
2-inch piece	fresh ginger, sliced	5-cm piece
1 bunch	cilantro (coriander leaves), minced	1 bunch
2 tbl	minced garlic	2 tbl
2 tbl	brown sugar	2 tbl
½ cup	water	125 ml
3 lb	pork tenderloins	1.4 kg
as needed	oil, for grill	as needed

1. Prepare marinade by mixing all ingredients except meat and oil for grill. Trim excess fat off pork, place pork in a bowl, and cover with marinade. Cover and let rest at least 2 hours at room temperature or up to 12 hours in the refrigerator.

2. Prepare fire for direct-heat method (see page 6). When fire is ready, remove meat from bowl, reserve excess marinade. Place tenderloins on oiled grill. Cook over hot fire, turning frequently. Baste often with reserved marinade. Tenderloins are done when lightly firm to the touch (145°F or 63°C on a meat thermometer), about 5 minutes.

Serves 4.

MICROWAVE-BOOSTED BARBECUE

A microwave oven and a grill make wonderful partners. When designing an outdoor cooking space, consider a microwave as a permanent appliance in that area. A microwave oven has so many uses for barbecuing and grilling, you'll be glad you have one for outdoor use. Here are some ways your microwave can help you cut down on grilling time:

- *Precook chicken, ribs, and other items in the microwave, then finish cooking on the grill.*

- *For medium or well-done steaks without burning, sear meat over hot coals and then microwave to order.*

- *Use microwave vegetable accompaniments such as baked beans or potatoes.*

- *Prepare barbecue sauce or other grilling condiments in the microwave.*

- *Grill extra burgers or steaks, then freeze and reheat in the microwave. This method works best for meats cooked medium to well-done.*

- *For a large group, barbecue chicken or burgers ahead and reheat in the microwave. This way everyone, including the chef, can be served at the same time.*

LAMB

Lamb is a natural for grilling because the excess fat drips off during cooking. Rib and loin chops are the most popular cuts for grilling, and butterflied leg of lamb is the all-time grilled roast classic. The chops are tender and require no marinade; the leg of lamb needs one to tenderize it. For tender, flavorful kabobs or skewers, use chunks from the shoulder or leg and marinate them. See page 15 for a tasty marinade for lamb.

ARMENIAN SHISH KABOB

The secret of preparing shish kabob meat is to bathe chunks of perfectly trimmed lamb in a simple olive oil marinade. See Timing Grilled Skewers (page 66).

2 lb	boneless leg of lamb, trimmed of all fat and cut in 2-inch (5 cm) cubes	900 g
½ cup	olive oil	125 ml
2 tbl	fresh lemon juice	2 tbl
3 cloves	garlic, peeled and crushed	3 cloves
1 tsp	dry white wine	1 tsp
1	bay leaf	1
pinch	salt	pinch
pinch	freshly ground black pepper	pinch
pinch	dried oregano	pinch
pinch	crumbled dried rosemary leaves	pinch
16	skewers	16
2	onions, peeled and cut into 8 wedges each	2
2	green bell peppers, cut into 8 pieces each	2
12	mushrooms, stemmed and wiped clean	12
2	tomatoes, cut into 8 wedges each, or 16 cherry tomatoes	2

1. Place lamb in a large container with a cover. In a medium bowl mix olive oil, lemon juice, garlic, wine, bay leaf, salt, pepper, oregano, and rosemary. Pour marinade over lamb cubes, stir thoroughly, and refrigerate, covered, at least 24 hours, stirring occasionally.

2. About 1 hour before serving time, prepare fire for direct-heat method (see page 6). Drain lamb kabobs, reserving marinade. Thread separate skewers of lamb, onion, green pepper, and mushrooms. Baste vegetables with some of reserved marinade. Grill about 4 inches (10 cm) from heat, turning frequently, as follows: lamb and green pepper, about 7 minutes; onions, about 12 minutes; mushrooms, about 3 minutes. Remove skewers and allow to cool slightly, until ingredients and skewers can be handled.

3. Remove skewers from ingredients and rethread 4 or 8 skewers (depending on size of skewers) so that each one includes lamb, onion, green pepper, mushrooms, and tomato. Baste again with any remaining marinade. Return skewers to grill and, turning frequently, cook until meat is reheated and cooked medium-rare, vegetables are slightly blackened in spots, and tomatoes are very tender (5–7 minutes more).

Serves 4.

SPICY LAMB CHOP GRILL

Grilled lamb chops are rich enough to be served without any accompaniment, but for a treat, serve them with this spicy sauce.

1	fresh jalapeño pepper	1
3 tbl	salad oil	3 tbl
1	onion, chopped	1
2	red bell peppers, chopped	2
2 cloves	garlic, chopped	2 cloves
1½ lb	ripe tomatoes, peeled, seeded, and chopped	680 g
to taste	salt and pepper	to taste
8	rib lamb chops, about 1½ inches (3.75 cm) thick	8

1. Discard seeds and ribs from jalapeño; chop pepper finely. Immediately wash your hands, cutting board, and knife.

2. In a deep frying pan over low heat, heat 2 tablespoons of the oil. Add onion; cook, stirring often, until soft but not browned (about 5 minutes). Add bell peppers, garlic, and jalapeño; cook, stirring often, until peppers soften (about 5 minutes).

3. Add tomatoes and a pinch of salt and raise heat to medium. Cook, uncovered, stirring often, until mixture is thick (about 30 minutes). Taste and add more salt, if needed. The sauce can be refrigerated, covered, for about 4 days, or frozen.

4. Prepare fire for direct-heat method (see page 6). Trim excess fat from chops, brush both sides with the remaining tablespoon of oil, and sprinkle them with salt and pepper. Put chops on hot grill; grill until done (about 6 minutes per side for medium-rare). To check for doneness, press meat with your finger. Rare lamb does not resist; medium-rare lamb resists slightly; well-done lamb is firm (see page 27).

5. Meanwhile, reheat sauce in a saucepan over medium heat. Transfer chops to platter. Serve sauce separately.

Serves 4.

BUTTERFLIED LEG O'LAMB

The short marination (only 4 hours), quick grill time, and refined presentation make this luscious leg of lamb an excellent choice for a weekend dinner.

1	onion	1
1 cup	plain yogurt	250 ml
1 tbl	minced garlic	1 tbl
1 bunch	cilantro (coriander leaves), stemmed and chopped	1 bunch
¼ cup	olive oil	60 ml
to taste	salt and pepper	to taste
7–8 lb	leg of lamb, boned and butterflied	3.2–3.6 kg
as needed	oil, for grill	as needed

Cucumber-Mint Sauce

1	cucumber	1
1	onion	1
1 tsp	minced garlic	1 tsp
¼ cup	chopped mint leaves	60 ml
1 cup	plain yogurt	250 ml
to taste	salt and pepper	to taste

1. Prepare marinade by puréeing onion in food processor or blender. Combine onion with yogurt, garlic, cilantro, olive oil, salt, and pepper.

2. Be sure to have a butcher bone and butterfly the leg of lamb to a uniform thickness. This is very important; otherwise, it will not cook evenly. The butcher should also trim the outside fat as closely as possible and remove all interior fat and connective tissue.

3. Rub the marinade into the meat and cover. Let rest at room temperature for at least 4 hours or refrigerate for up to 12 hours.

4. To prepare Cucumber-Mint Sauce, peel cucumber, quarter lengthwise, and slice thin. Peel and finely dice onion and combine with cucumber, garlic, mint, and yogurt. Adjust seasoning with salt and pepper. Chill before serving.

5. Prepare fire for indirect-heat method (see page 6). Wipe excess marinade from meat and reserve marinade remaining in bowl. When fire is ready, sear both sides of meat over direct heat on oiled grill, then place lamb, skin side down, over drip pan and close lid.

6. You don't need to turn the lamb over during cooking. Baste occasionally with reserved marinade. Cook until meat is rare (140°F or 60°C), about 45 minutes. Remove from grill and cover with foil. Allow to rest for 10 minutes for juices to collect in meat. To serve cut across the grain. Serve with Cucumber-Mint Sauce.

Serves 8.

POULTRY

Poultry is one of the most versatile foods for grilling, accepting almost any marinade or sauce with beautiful results. Fresh chicken—fryers or broilers weighing 3–4 pounds (1.4–1.8 kg)—can easily be grilled over direct heat (see page 6) if split, quartered, or cut into pieces. Game hens, whole or butterflied, can be grilled using direct heat. Turkey breast fillets are ideal for direct-heat cooking. To grill a whole chicken, turkey, or duck, use the indirect-heat method of cooking (see page 6).

GEORGIA CHICKEN

Georgia-style barbecue sauce and slow cooking gives chicken a sweet, mild flavor. Serve with pasta salad or coleslaw, corn on the cob, lemonade, and peach pie.

3 cups	Georgia Barbecue Sauce, (see page19)	700 ml
3–4 lb	1 chicken, in pieces	1.4–1.8 kg
¼ cup	oil	60 ml

1. Prepare Georgia Barbecue Sauce.

2. Prepare fire for indirect-heat method (see page 6). Wash chicken and pat dry. Lightly coat with oil.

3. When fire is ready, add hardwood chips or chunks if using charcoal or gas grill. Allow grill temperature to cool to 225°F (110°C). Lightly sear chicken on all sides over direct heat, about 5 minutes per side. Move chicken over indirect heat and close lid. Monitor fire to maintain proper cooking temperature. After 15 minutes, turn chicken over. Use half the sauce for basting and reserve remainder to serve at the table.

4. After another 15 minutes place a piece of heavy-duty foil under chicken. Prick foil with fork in 12 places to allow smoke to penetrate meat. Baste chicken with sauce. Close lid. Every 10 minutes, baste chicken and turn. Chicken is done in 45 minutes–1 hour of total cooking time. Serve immediately with reserved hot barbecue sauce.

Serves 3 or 4.

CHICKEN SATAY

A sweet and peppery peanut sauce tenderizes these Indonesian chicken strips grilled with red peppers until crisp and juicy.

3	whole chicken breasts, boned, skinned, and halved	3
1 cup	crunchy peanut butter	250 ml
⅓ cup	chopped cilantro (coriander leaves)	85 ml
½ cup	chili sauce	125 ml
1 tbl	salt	1 tbl
½ tsp	cayenne pepper	½ tsp
½ tsp	freshly ground black pepper	½ tsp
¼ cup	lemon juice	60 ml
¼ cup	brown sugar	60 ml
½ cup	soy sauce	125 ml
8	green onions, minced	8
3 tbl	minced garlic	3 tbl
24	skewers	24
2	sweet bell peppers, red or green, cut into ½-inch (1.25 cm) cubes	2
as needed	minced parsley, for garnish	as needed

1. Slice each half-breast into four lengthwise strips. Set aside.

2. In a stainless steel or glass bowl, combine all ingredients except for bell peppers and parsley. Add chicken strips, cover, and let marinate overnight or up to 2 days.

3. Prepare fire for direct-heat method (see page 6). Thread chicken strips onto skewers in spiral fashion, with pepper cubes interspersed. Grill for 5–6 minutes, turning once. Serve garnished with minced parsley.

Makes 24 cocktail kabobs.

HERBAL SKEWERS

The best skewers for flavorful grilled kabobs may be right under your nose. In late summer and early fall many aromatic herbs such as basil, mint, rosemary, and tarragon develop woody stalks you can transform into herbal skewers that flavor food from the inside out.

1. Remove leaves from woody stalks and use a paring knife to sharpen one end of each stalk so that it can pierce the food.

2. Soak the stalks briefly in water; then thread with pieces of meat, vegetables, or fruit and grill to taste.

3. For a festive presentation, serve kabobs with the herbal skewers intact.

Pollo Pequeño

This spicy multi-napkin nibble makes a tasty appetizer to eat while the rest of the meal grills. Save the wing tips for chicken stock.

½ cup	dry sherry	125 ml
2 tbl	sherry vinegar	2 tbl
2 tbl	lemon juice	2 tbl
1 tbl	tomato paste	1 tbl
1 tbl	sugar	1 tbl
2 tbl	minced garlic	2 tbl
2 tsp	salt	2 tsp
2 tbl	ground cumin	2 tbl
½ tsp	cayenne pepper	½ tsp
24	chicken wings, tips removed	24
2 tbl	chopped cilantro (coriander leaves), for garnish	2 tbl

1. In stainless steel or glass bowl, combine all ingredients except chicken and cilantro. Marinate chicken in mixture for at least 4 hours or overnight.

2. Prepare fire for direct-heat method (see page 6). When fire is ready, place chicken on grill. Cook and baste for 12–15 minutes, until crisp and richly browned.

3. Serve hot, garnished with chopped cilantro.

Makes 24.

When Is Poultry Done?

Use a thermometer or visual clues to test for doneness:

- *An instant-read thermometer inserted into the thickest part of the breast (not touching the breastbone) should register 170°–175°F (77°–80°C).*

- *The flesh should spring back slightly when lightly touched.*

- *The leg joint should move easily in its socket.*

LEMON-BASTED CHICKEN

Use mesquite chunks to complement the lemon garlic flavor of the chicken, and serve with roasted red peppers (see pages 84–85).

4 lb	chicken, whole	1.8 kg
2	lemons	2
1 tbl	minced garlic	1 tbl
to taste	salt and pepper	to taste
2–3 tbl	olive oil	2–3 tbl
as needed	oil, for grill	as needed

1. Wash chicken thoroughly and pat dry. Peel lemons and dice the rind. Juice both lemons.

2. To make basting mixture, combine one half the lemon rind with garlic, salt and pepper, lemon juice, and olive oil. Coat chicken inside and out with basting mixture; reserve remainder. Stuff chicken cavity with remaining lemon rind.

3. Prepare fire for indirect-heat method (see page 6). When fire is ready, place chicken on oiled grill directly over heat. Sear chicken on all sides, then place over drip pan, breast side up. Close lid. Cook for 1–1½ hours, basting occasionally with reserved basting mixture. Chicken is done when juices run slightly pink to clear, or when an instant-read thermometer reads about 165°F (74°C). Serve hot or cover and refrigerate and serve cold.

Serves 4.

GRILLED ROCK CORNISH GAME HENS

In this recipe, the game hens are butterflied for ease of handling and quick cooking. See Flavoring the Fire (below).

2 tbl	butter, softened	2 tbl
2 tbl	minced shallots	2 tbl
1 lb each	2 Rock Cornish game hens	450 g each
to taste	salt	to taste

1. In a small bowl combine butter and shallots until well blended. Set aside.

2. Cut along backbone of game hens with poultry shears. Open up birds to create a butterfly effect. Lightly salt both sides.

3. Prepare fire for direct-heat method (see page 6). When coals are ready, place game hens, breast side down, on grill; sear. Turn; sear other side. Grill game hens, brushing frequently with the shallot butter, until the flesh springs back slightly when touched (about 10–12 minutes).

Serves 2.

FLAVORING THE FIRE

Adding hardwood chunks or chips is one way to flavor a fire, but you can also experiment with fresh cuttings of bay, lavender, marjoram, oregano, rosemary, thyme, or other herbs.

1. *If using herbs, trim cuttings to fit grill.*

2. *Use water, wine, or liquor to moisten cuttings; then toss onto the hot coals just before you put food on the grill. The cuttings will quickly begin to produce smoke.*

3. *Grill as usual. Avoid directly inhaling the fumes,*

GRILLED BREAST OF DUCK

Who says grilled food always has to be casual? This impressive duck grill is easy and fast. Serve with rice, steamed asparagus, and a cabernet or Merlot for a sophisticated supper.

2 tbl	olive oil	2 tbl
1 lb	red or yellow onions, thinly sliced	450 g
1 cup	dry red wine	250 ml
1 tsp	honey	1 tsp
1 sprig	fresh thyme	1 sprig
1	bay leaf	1
2	whole duck breasts, skinned, boned, and split	2
to taste	salt and freshly ground black pepper	to taste

1. Prepare fire for direct-heat method (see page 6).

2. Heat oil in a heavy saucepan over medium heat. Add sliced onions and cook, stirring frequently, until they begin to wilt. Do not brown.

3. Add wine, honey, thyme, and bay leaf. Bring sauce to a boil, reduce to a simmer, and cook until onions soften, about 20 minutes. Set sauce aside and keep warm.

4. Season duck breasts with salt and pepper and grill to the medium-rare stage, 3–4 minutes per side. Serve the breasts on top of the onion sauce.

Serves 4.

Note *Ducks make wonderful grilled fare. They freeze well, so if you can't find them fresh, feel confident with using frozen ducks for grilling. Whole ducks should be cooked over indirect heat because of their high fat content. Prick the skin all over with a fork to allow the fat to drip out and moisten the duck as it roasts.*

Cilantro-Turkey Fillets

The cilantro butter seasons the turkey and keeps it moist as it grills.

1 recipe	Salsa Cruda (see page 31)	1 recipe
¼ cup	butter, softened	60 ml
½ cup	minced cilantro (coriander leaves)	125 ml
4	turkey fillets, halved lengthwise	4

1. Prepare the salsa and set aside.

2. In a small bowl combine softened butter with cilantro. Set aside. Wash turkey fillets and pat dry.

3. Prepare fire for direct-heat method (see page 6). When coals are ready, sear fillets. Grill 5 inches (12.5 cm) from heat, brushing both sides of fillet with cilantro butter, about 8 minutes total cooking time.

4. Serve dotted with remaining cilantro butter and Salsa Cruda.

Serves 6 to 8.

Safety Tips for Fresh Poultry

Because fresh poultry is extremely perishable and may carry potentially harmful organisms, it must be handled with care.

- *Store in the coldest part of the refrigerator and use as soon as possible, within 1–2 days of purchase.*

- *Four hours is the maximum time raw or cooked poultry can safely be left at room temperature.*

- *Thoroughly wash and dry raw poultry before using.*

- *The safest way to thaw frozen poultry is in the refrigerator.*

- *Wash hands, work surfaces, and utensils in hot, soapy water before and after contact with raw poultry.*

- *Cook poultry thoroughly. See page 56.*

SEAFOOD

Fish is the ideal medium for direct-heat cooking. The tender flesh has no tough connective tissue, and most varieties contain enough fat to stay succulent on the grill. Low in fat and palate-pleasing, all seafood is best when it is at its freshest. Shellfish are among the world's best-loved foods, but remember that all shellfish deteriorate rapidly after harvesting. Buy only from a reputable dealer with a rapid turnover, and keep fresh shellfish refrigerated on a bed of ice, loosely covered with a clean towel.

GRILLED LOBSTER WITH GARDEN VINAIGRETTE

A chunky vinaigrette is an enticing alternative to butter sauces.

Garden Vinaigrette

2 tbl	apple cider vinegar	2 tbl
1 tbl	lemon juice	1 tbl
1 tsp	Dijon mustard	1 tsp
2 tbl	minced parsley	2 tbl
¾ cup	olive oil	175 ml
½ cup	diced fresh tomato	125 ml
2 tsp	minced chives	2 tsp
to taste	salt and freshly ground black pepper	to taste
2 lb each	2 live lobsters	900 g each
¼ cup	melted unsalted butter	60 ml

1. To prepare Garden Vinaigrette, whisk together vinegar, lemon juice, mustard, and parsley in a medium bowl. Add oil in a slow, steady stream, whisking constantly; mixture should be thick and creamy. Stir in tomatoes and chives. Season to taste with salt and pepper and set aside.

2. Bring a large pot of salted water to a boil over high heat. Plunge lobsters into boiling water for 2 minutes. Drain. When lobsters are cool enough to handle, split them in half lengthwise with a heavy knife. Remove and discard any viscera, including the intestinal vein in the tail.

3. Prepare fire for direct-heat method (see page 6). Brush lobsters with melted butter and place them on grill, shell side up. Grill over a medium-hot fire for 8–10 minutes, then turn, brush with butter, and continue grilling until tails are firm and white (about 5 minutes more). Remove to a warm serving platter. Twist off claws and return the claws to grill for an additional 3–4 minutes. Serve on platter accompanied by vinaigrette sauce.

Serves 4.

OYSTERS MIGNONETTE

Piquant Mignonette Sauce adds zip to grilled oysters. Keep in mind that during cooking oysters open only a crack, not wide like clams.

Mignonette Sauce

¾ cup	white wine vinegar	175 ml
¾ cup	dry white wine	175 ml
3	shallots, minced	3
1 tsp	freshly ground black pepper	1 tsp
2 tsp	minced parsley	2 tsp
24	oysters in the shell	24
2	onions	2
2 heads	radicchio	2 heads
as needed	olive oil, for brushing	as needed

1. To prepare Mignonette Sauce, in a medium bowl combine all ingredients and mix well.

2. To prepare oysters, prepare fire for direct-heat method (see page 6). Scrub oysters. Place them with the deeper shell on grill. When oysters open, remove them from grill.

3. To prepare onions and radicchio, peel onions and slice in half, leaving core intact to hold onion together. Brush vegetables with olive oil and grill until radicchio begins to wilt and onions begin to soften.

4. Serve oysters on a platter with Mignonette Sauce in the center and onions and radicchio on the side.

Serves 6 to 8.

GRILLING TIMES FOR FISH

The rules of thumb for cooking any fish, by any method, include placing the grill 4–6 inches above the heat source and cooking the fish for 10 minutes per inch of thickness. A hot fire and short cooking time are essential for succulent grilled fish. Exact cooking times are difficult to predict because of the variability of the factors involved—the heat of the coals, the distance between the coals and the grill, and the type of coals. See Tips for Grilling Fish (page 71).

MEXICAN-STYLE SHRIMP SKEWERS

These splendidly garlicky shrimp need only 3 minutes on the grill. See Timing Grilled Skewers (below).

1½ lb	medium to large shrimp	680g
5 tbl	butter	5 tbl
3 cloves	garlic, pressed	3 cloves
pinch	mild powdered chile, unseasoned	pinch
1 tbl	fresh lime juice	1 tbl
24	skewers	24

1. Peel and devein shrimp, leaving tails on.

2. Prepare fire for direct-heat method (see page 6).

3. Melt butter in a small pan. Add remaining ingredients. Simmer 1 minute.

4. Dip each shrimp in garlic butter and place on skewers. Grill over hot coals, basting with the remaining garlic butter, turning once and cooking only until pink (approximately 3 minutes). Do not overcook the shrimp or they will toughen.

Serves 4 as a main course, or 6 to 8 as an appetizer.

TIMING GRILLED SKEWERS

When combining vegetables with meat or fish on skewers, try to select foods that will cook in the same amount of time. For example, shrimp cooks quickly, so pick vegetables such as green onions, mushrooms, and cherry tomatoes that also cook quickly. If you want to add onions, blanch them first or grill until partially done, since they require a longer cooking time than the shrimp. Or, if you grill meat that takes longer to cook, choose your vegetables accordingly. For 1-inch (2.5 cm) cubes of beef, use raw pieces of bell pepper, onion, or zucchini.

CREOLE KABOBS

Serve this Gulf Coast mixed grill as an hors d'oeuvre or main course.

Mustard Butter

1 cup	unsalted butter	250 ml
2 tbl	minced garlic	2 tbl
3 tbl	coarse-grained mustard	3 tbl
2 tsp	Worcestershire sauce	2 tsp
1 tsp	hot pepper sauce	1 tsp
⅓ cup	lemon juice	85 ml
to taste	salt and pepper	to taste
24	skewers	24
1 each	red and greenbell pepper, cut into 1-inch (2.5 cm) chunks	1 each
1	red onion, cut into 1-inch (2.5 cm) chunks	1
1 lb	large shrimp with tails, peeled and deveined	450 g
as needed	oil, for grill	as needed
1 lb	Andouille or Polish sausage, cut into ½-inch-thick (1.25 cm) rounds	450 g

1. To prepare Mustard Butter, melt butter in a small saucepan. Add garlic and whisk in mustard, Worcestershire, hot pepper sauce, and lemon juice. Season with salt and pepper. Butter can be used at this point or chilled and remelted later.

2. Thread ingredients onto skewers, pushing skewers through the length of the shrimp and through casing side of sausage so the cut edge is parallel with the skewer.

3. Prepare fire for direct heat method (see page 6). When fire is ready, brush skewers with Mustard Butter, place on oiled grill over heat, and cook 2–3 minutes per side. Serve with remaining Mustard Butter.

Serves 12 as an appetizer; 6 as a main course.

GRILLED LEMON-PEPPER CLAMS

Although clams make great stand-up cocktail food, you can also serve them as a first course at the table. Try the tangy Lemon-Pepper Vinegar drizzled on raw clams or oysters on the half shell.

Lemon-Pepper Vinegar

2 tsp	grated lemon zest	2 tsp
2 tsp	coarsely cracked black peppercorns	2 tsp
1 cup	apple cider vinegar	250 ml
24	small clams	24
2 tbl	cornmeal	2 tbl
¼ cup	unsalted butter, melted	60 ml

1. To prepare Lemon-Pepper Vinegar, whisk all ingredients together in a small bowl and set aside..

2. Place clams in a stainless steel or glass bowl. Add cornmeal and water to cover. Refrigerate at least 4 hours or up to 12 hours to allow clams to disgorge any sand.

3. Prepare fire for direct-heat method (see page 6). When coals are medium-hot and gray, drain clams and place on grill, as close to coals as possible. As clams open (3–5 minutes), remove to a warm serving bowl and brush clam meat with melted butter. Discard any clams that do not open after 5 minutes. Serve immediately with Lemon-Pepper Vinegar.

Serves 4 as an appetizer, 3 as a first course.

DILLED SALMON STEAKS

Herb butter complements the savory goodness of one of the finest fish for grilling (see photo on page 12).

Green Onion-Dill Butter

½ cup	unsalted butter, softened	125 ml
4 tbl	fresh dill, minced	4 tbl
2	green onions, minced	2
2 tbl	lime juice	2 tbl
¼ tsp	cayenne pepper	¼ tsp
½ tsp	salt	½ tsp
8 oz each	6 salmon steaks	225 g each
as needed	oil, for grilling	as needed

1. To prepare Green-Onion Dill Butter, in small bowl stir together all ingredients and set aside.

2. Prepare fire for direct-heat method (see page 6). Baste fish with oil to reduce charring. Grill fish for 5 minutes, brush other side with oil, turn, and grill 5–8 minutes more, depending on thickness.

3. Top each steak with 1 tablespoon Green Onion-Dill Butter.

Serves 6.

TIPS FOR GRILLING FISH

- *To prevent flare-ups from oily marinades, arrange hot coals to outline the fish, leaving only ashes directly under the fish.*

- *To keep delicate fillets or whole fish intact while turning, use a hinged grill basket. Place basket on grill, heat, and oil lightly before placing fish inside.*

- *As soon as the fish is done, serve it immediately on hot plates.*

Grilled Fish Diablo

Oven-roasted potatoes and a bottle of dry white Bordeaux transform this easy fish grill into a complete dinner. Try substituting a green and a yellow bell pepper for two of the reds.

3	red bell peppers	3
7 tbl	olive oil	7 tbl
1 tsp	minced fresh thyme	1 tsp
1½ tbl	minced garlic	1½ tbl
2 tbl	capers	2 tbl
to taste	salt and freshly ground black pepper	to taste
to taste	cayenne pepper	to taste
2 tbl	lemon juice	2 tbl
pinch	hot-pepper flakes	pinch
6–8 oz each	6 fillets rock cod	170–225 g each
	or other firm-fleshed white fish	

1. Halve bell peppers, remove stems, ribs, and seeds, and cut into ¼-inch-wide (.6 cm) strips. In a large skillet over moderate heat, heat 4 tablespoons of the olive oil. Add peppers and stir to coat with oil. Add thyme, cover, and cook for 10 minutes. Uncover, add garlic and capers, and raise heat to high. Sauté for 30 seconds, stirring. Remove from heat. Season to taste with salt, black pepper, and cayenne.

2. Prepare fire for direct-heat method (see page 6). Thirty minutes before fire is ready, whisk together the remaining 3 tablespoons olive oil, lemon juice, and pepper flakes. Brush fish with some of the mixture. Let stand at room temperature until ready to cook. Salt and pepper fish lightly, then grill to desired doneness (8–10 minutes per inch or 2.5 cm of thickness), basting occasionally with remaining marinade. You do not need to turn fish. Serve immediately, topped with warm peppers.

Serves 6.

MESQUITE-GRILLED SWORDFISH

Fresh swordfish needs nothing more than a light coating of olive oil while it grills and a touch of Cilantro Butter after it's done. Mesquite, which burns very hot, is especially good for grilling swordfish.

Cilantro Butter

1 bunch	cilantro (coriander leaves)	1 bunch
½ cup	unsalted butter	125 ml
¼ cup	lemon juice	60 ml
to taste	salt and pepper	to taste
8 oz each	4 fresh swordfish center-cut fillets	225 g each
2 tbl	olive oil	2 tbl
as needed	oil, for grill	as needed

1. To prepare Cilantro Butter, wash cilantro and remove thick stems. Combine with butter in food processor or blender and process several seconds until light and fluffy. Blend in lemon juice. Add salt and pepper to taste.

2. Prepare fire for direct-heat method (see page 6).

3. Wash fish and pat dry. Lightly coat fillets with olive oil.

4. When fire is ready, place fish on oiled grill and cook until done (about 4 minutes per side for thick fillets). Serve immediately with Cilantro Butter.

Serves 4.

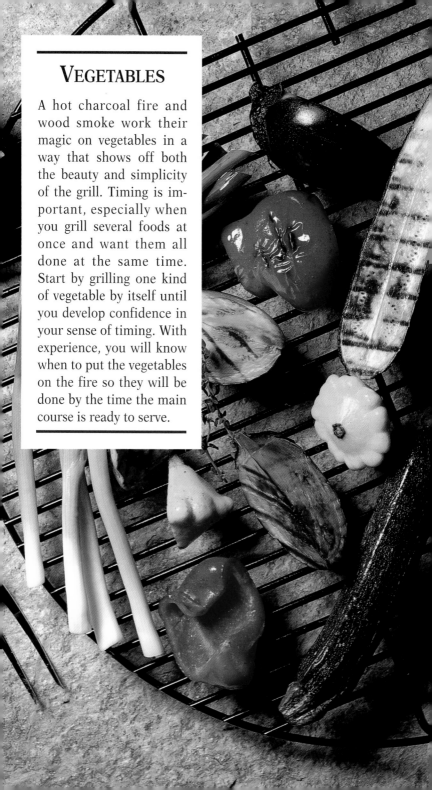

VEGETABLES

A hot charcoal fire and wood smoke work their magic on vegetables in a way that shows off both the beauty and simplicity of the grill. Timing is important, especially when you grill several foods at once and want them all done at the same time. Start by grilling one kind of vegetable by itself until you develop confidence in your sense of timing. With experience, you will know when to put the vegetables on the fire so they will be done by the time the main course is ready to serve.

VEGETABLE MIXED GRILL

The garlic rubdown and the lemon juice give these vegetables enough zip to be served without a sauce, but if you're feeling indulgent, fresh aioli (garlic-laced mayonnaise) or clarified butter makes a fine accompaniment. See Preparing Eggplant for the Grill (page 79).

1 lb	eggplant (see page 79)	450 g
1 lb	zucchini	450 g
1 lb	yellow pattypan squash	450 g
2	red bell peppers	2
1 bunch	green onions	1 bunch
½ cup	olive oil	125 ml
2 tbl	minced garlic	2 tbl
to taste	salt and pepper	to taste
1	lemon (optional)	1

1. Wash all vegetables and pat dry. Cut eggplant and zucchini lengthwise into 1-inch-thick (2.5 cm) slices. Quarter patty-pan squash. Cut peppers lengthwise into quarters and remove seeds. Remove roots from green onions.

2. On a baking sheet mix oil, garlic, and salt and pepper. Rub vegetables with oil mixture.

3. Prepare fire for direct-heat method (see page 6). Use presoaked hardwood chips or chunks for a smoky flavor. When fire is ready, place vegetables on grill and close lid immediately to control flare-ups from oil.

4. After 5–6 minutes, turn vegetables over. Brush with extra oil if surfaces appear to be drying out rather than cooking. Close lid. Vegetables should be done in another 5–6 minutes. Squeeze fresh lemon juice over vegetables and serve immediately.

Serves 3 or 4.

GRILLED VEGETABLE FAJITAS

Traditionally made with beef or chicken, these low-fat vegetable fajitas are given a quick grilling before being served with fresh salsa. See Timing Grilled Skewers (page 66) and Preparing Eggplant for the Grill (page 79).

12	skewers	12
1	eggplant, in ¾-inch (1.9 cm) cubes, (see page 79)	1
1	green bell pepper, halved, deribbed, seeded, and cut into 1-inch (2.5 cm) squares	1
½	red onion, cubed	½
½ pt	cherry tomatoes	225 ml
½ lb	zucchini, in ½-inch (1.25 cm) chunks	225 g
½ lb	small mushrooms	225 g
¼ cup	olive oil	60 ml
2 tbl	vegetable oil	2 tbl
to taste	salt and freshly ground black pepper	to taste
12	6 in. (15 cm) corn tortillas	12
as needed	Salsa Cruda (see page 31)	as needed

1. Prepare fire for direct-heat method (see page 6). Thread skewers, alternating vegetables. Whisk together olive oil and vegetable oil; season with salt and pepper. Drizzle seasoned oil over vegetables.

3. Grill vegetables, basting with seasoned oil, until lightly charred and softened (5–7 minutes). Heat tortillas on charcoal grill. To serve, push vegetables off skewers onto hot tortillas and top with Salsa Cruda.

Serves 4 (3 fajitas each).

GRILLED JAPANESE EGGPLANT

Japanese eggplant is ideal for grilling. It is thin enough to be grilled whole, and the skin browns beautifully, forming a tight seal that keeps the flesh moist as it cooks.

2 lb	6 Japanese eggplant	900 g
2 tbl	olive oil	2 tbl
1 tsp	minced garlic	1 tsp
to taste	salt and pepper	to taste

1. Wash eggplant and pat dry. Lightly coat with olive oil, garlic, and salt and pepper.

2. Prepare fire for direct-heat method (see page 6). When fire is ready, place eggplant over direct heat and close lid. Turn several times during cooking. Eggplant should be done in about 5 minutes.

Serves 4 to 6.

PREPARING EGGPLANT FOR THE GRILL

Western varieties of eggplant are larger and more globular than Japanese, Chinese, or Thai varieties, and have a high moisture content that can make them bitter. The Asian varieties need no special preparation before grilling. Pressing out the bitter juices of large globe eggplant before cooking can improve the flavor.

1. Wash and trim stem ends; do not peel.

2. Slice crosswise into slices ³/₄-inch (1.9 cm) and salt them liberally.

3. Press slices for one hour between sheets of toweling, weighted with a heavy plate or breadboard.

4. Rinse and pat dry; grill according to recipe.

SWEET CORN WITH CHILE-LIME BUTTER

This presentation is festive and fun, but you need the freshest corn possible for the best results. You can bury the corn for 30 minutes in coals producing low heat, but it's easier to cook—and avoid overcooking—by roasting the corn on top of the grill.

6	ears sweet corn, in husks	6
as needed	oil, for grill	as needed

Chile-Lime Butter

¾–1 cup	butter, at room temperature	175–250 ml
¼ cup	fresh lime juice	60 ml
2–3 tbl	chile powder	2–3 tbl
to taste	salt	to taste

1. Soak ears in cold water for at least 20 minutes.

2. Prepare fire for direct-heat method (see page 6).

3. To prepare Chile-Lime Butter, use fork to beat together all ingredients, adjusting proportions to taste.

4. When fire is ready, squeeze out excess water from ears, and lay them on grill. Corn cooks by steaming inside husks. Turn ears occasionally. Corn is done when husks are evenly browned (15–20 minutes).

5. When ready to serve, remove husks and silk and coat corn with Chile-Lime Butter.

Serves 6.

GRILLED POLENTA

Grilled polenta is crusty on the outside, creamy on the inside. Try substituting grilled grits for polenta at your next southern barbecue.

4 cups	water	900 ml
2 tsp	salt	2 tsp
1 cup	polenta	250 ml
6 tbl	unsalted butter	6 tbl
½ cup	grated Parmesan cheese	125 ml
¼ cup	olive oil	60 ml
as needed	oil, for grill	as needed

1. In a large pot on the stove, bring water and salt to a boil. Add polenta and stir constantly until polenta begins to thicken. Reduce heat to low and slowly cook for 20–30 minutes, stirring occasionally, until thick and creamy. Stir in butter and Parmesan cheese and remove from heat.

2. Pour polenta into a 10- by 14-inch (25- by 35-cm) heatproof dish, spreading evenly to about 1 inch (2.5 cm) thick. Chill in refrigerator, 1–2 hours (or in freezer, about 30 minutes).

3. Prepare fire for direct-heat method (see page 6). Cut polenta into 3-inch (7.5 cm) squares. Remove slices from dish and lightly coat both sides with olive oil. When fire is ready, place squares on oiled grill. Flip over when one side is brown (about 5 minutes). Remove from fire when other side is golden brown (about 5 minutes more). Serve immediately.

Serves 6.

ROASTED RED PEPPERS

The sweet, intense flavor of roasted red peppers adds piquancy to salads, sauces, stuffings, and grilled meats and poultry, such as Lemon-Basted Chicken (see recipe on page 56).

4	red bell peppers	4
2 tbl	olive oil	2 tbl
as needed	oil, for grill	as needed

1. Carefully cut away stems and wash red bell peppers. Peppers must be kept whole, so be careful not to split them. Remove seeds. Pat dry and coat peppers with olive oil.

2. Prepare fire for direct-heat method (see page 6). Using oven mitts and long tongs, place peppers on oiled grill over direct flame, turning often to char (not burn) the skins.

3. When peppers are uniformly charred, (3–5 minutes, depending on the intensity of the fire), immediately remove from heat and place in a heavy-duty paper bag, close tightly, and let rest for 10 minutes to allow the peppers to sweat.

4. Open bag and empty peppers onto cutting surface. Let cool slightly until you can touch them with your hands. Peel off most of charred skin from peppers, scraping stubborn spots with a knife. Place peppers in a bowl to collect juices that ooze out as peppers cool.

5. Serve at once. To store, leave peppers in bowl, soak with additional olive oil, cover, and leave in a cool place for up to several weeks.

Makes 1 cup (250 ml).

ROASTED GARLIC

Serve as an appetizer, squeezing the buttery cloves out of their skins and spreading over slices of French bread.

6 heads	garlic, unpeeled	6 heads
¼ cup	olive oil	60 ml
4 tbl	unsalted butter	4 tbl
4 sprigs	fresh oregano	4 sprigs
1 baguette	French bread	1 baguette

1. Prepare fire for indirect-heat method (see page 6).

2. Cut the top end off the garlic heads, exposing individual cloves. Place the heads in a piece of foil and drizzle with olive oil. Butter lightly and add oregano. Tightly seal foil. Place on grill in a spot not directly over the coals.

3. After about 45 minutes, open packet and baste heads with juices from packet. Reseal and roast until spreadably soft (about 45 minutes more). Remove packet from grill and serve.

Serves 4 to 6.

KIDS COOKING AT THE GRILL

When is a child old enough to cook over a grill? Each child is different. Some may be ready at six years old; others may be teenagers before they are ready. If a child is interested and tall enough to easily reach the grill, he or she is probably ready to try grilling simple foods such as hot dogs, burgers, corn on the cob, or skewered foods.

Be sure to start the fire yourself and stay close by throughout the entire cooking process. Offer help when it's genuinely needed, but let kids do the cooking themselves. There's no better teacher than experience when it comes to barbecuing and grilling.

GARDEN BURGERS

The next time you're thinking of grilling burgers with all the fixings, try this tasty, low-fat vegetarian version. Serve with your favorite barbecue sauce and accompaniments.

¼ cup	bulgur	60 ml
1 cup	boiling water	250 ml
1	onion, minced	1
3 cloves	garlic, minced	3 cloves
15–18 sprigs	parsley, minced	15–18 sprigs
2	eggs	2
3 cups	cooked garbanzos (chick peas)	700 ml
2 tbl	plain yogurt	2 tbl
1 tsp	salt	1 tsp
½ tsp	coarsely ground black pepper	½ tsp
½ tsp	cumin	½ tsp
½ tsp	cayenne pepper	½ tsp
½ cup	bread crumbs	125 ml
as needed	oil, for grill	as needed

1. Place bulgur in a 1-quart (900 ml) bowl, and cover with the water. Let rest for 30 minutes. Drain.

2. Place bulgur and remaining ingredients except bread crumbs and oil in a blender or food processor. Process to a smooth paste.

3. Shape ½ cup (125 ml) of mixture at a time into burgers and pat on bread crumbs. Chill for 1 hour.

4. Place burgers on hot oiled grill and cook for 3 minutes. Turn and cook on second side for 3 minutes more.

Serves 8.

FRUIT

Whether as an appetizer, a side dish, or a sweet finale to a meal, many varieties of fruit take naturally to the grill. Grilling enhances the aroma and sweetness of apples, bananas, cherries, figs, grapefruit, kiwi, nectarines, oranges, mangoes, peaches, strawberries, tangerines, cantaloupe, pineapple, and other fruits.

Jamaican Banana Grill

The bananas are bathed in a light rum syrup after grilling. Make this dessert close to serving time, so the bananas retain their shape and fresh taste.

6	bananas, unpeeled	6
1 tsp	butter	1 tsp
½ cup	apple juice	125 ml
½ cup	white rum	125 ml
¼ cup	brown sugar	60 ml
½ tsp	nutmeg	½ tsp

1. Prepare fire for indirect-heat method (see page 6). When fire is ready, place unpeeled bananas on grill. Prick the skin of each banana several times with the prongs of a fork. Grill bananas, turning often, until skins turn black (about 10 minutes).

2. In a large skillet combine remaining ingredients and cook over medium-high heat on stove or atop grill for 8 minutes until mixture is syrupy.

3. Carefully peel each banana, cut in half lengthwise, and place in the rum syrup. Grilled bananas are delicate, so handle carefully. Cook, turning once, until lightly golden (about 2 minutes). Serve warm.

Serves 6.

Pineapple-Citrus Skewers

Substitute blueberries or any other fresh berries for the raspberry garnish.

8	skewers	8
1	fresh pineapple, cut into	1
	1-inch (2.5 cm) chunks	
2	oranges, peeled and divided into wedges	2
3 tbl	butter, melted	3 tbl
2 tbl	light brown sugar	2 tbl
	oil, for the grill	
2 cups	fresh raspberries, for garnish	500 ml

1. Thread skewers alternately with the pineapple and orange slices. Mix butter with the sugar and brush over skewered fruit.

2. Prepare fire for direct-heat method (see page 6). When fire is ready, lightly oil grill. Place kabobs on the grill and cook for 3–5 minutes, turning often, until lightly browned.

3. To serve, place a skewer on each dessert dish and garnish with raspberries.

Makes 8.

TIPS FOR GRILLING FRUIT

- Most fruits can be grilled with the peel left on; remove the skin from cantaloupe, kiwis, and pineapple before grilling.

- If desired, marinate fruits in white or red wine or fruit juice to which you've added chopped fresh mint leaves.

- Use a medium to hot fire.

- Grill just long enough to bring out the aroma and flavor of whatever fruit you're grilling. Remove from the grill when the color of the fruit changes slightly and you see grill marks or light charring around the edges.

- Serve plain or with crushed fruit, a cream sauce flavored with chocolate or liqueur, a spoonful of ice cream or frozen yogurt, or an assortment of cheeses.

GRILLED FRUIT KABOBS

This is an elegant grilled variation on fresh fruit salad. The sour cream sauce, deliciously flavored with nutmeg and honey, can be made ahead and stored in a tightly covered container in the refrigerator for up to one week. For a savory version, alternate cubes of firm-bodied cheese (Cheddar, Edam, or fontina) with the fruit, grill as usual, and omit the sweet sauce.

Sour Cream Sauce

¾ cup	nonfat plain yogurt	175 ml
¼ cup	sour cream	60 ml
2 tsp	freshly grated nutmeg	2 tsp
1 tbl	maple syrup	1 tbl
1 tbl	honey	1 tbl
as needed	fresh mint leaves, for garnish	as needed
¾ cup each	papaya cubes, pineapple chunks, sliced bananas, peach chunks, and whole strawberries	175 ml each
12	skewers	12

1. For Sour Cream Sauce, mix together all ingredients except garnish and pour into a small serving bowl. Garnish with mint leaves.

2. Prepare fire for direct-heat method (see page 6). Thread fruit onto skewers, alternating colors and varieties. Grill over hot coals until lightly browned, turning once. Remove from grill and arrange on a platter. Serve with Sour Cream Sauce.

Makes 12 skewers.

GINGERED GRILLED MELON

First marinated in ginger, then seasoned with pepper and lemon, lightly grilled melon makes a refreshing finish to any meal. A scoop of ice cream or frozen yogurt turns it into a special dessert.

1	cantaloupe or honeydew melon, barely ripe	1
2 tbl	minced crystallized ginger	2 tbl
2 tbl	minced fresh ginger	2 tbl
½ cup	rice wine	125 ml
pinch	sugar	pinch
pinch	salt	pinch
½	cinnamon stick	½
to taste	white pepper	to taste
to taste	lemon juice	to taste

1. Peel and quarter melon; cut each quarter into 4 slices.

2. In a small saucepan combine 1 tablespoon crystallized ginger, the fresh ginger, wine, sugar, salt, and cinnamon stick. Bring to a simmer on stove or atop grill. Remove from heat and add melon. Allow melon to marinate in liquid until the liquid is cool.

3. Remove melon and strain liquid through a fine sieve. In a small saucepan over high heat, reduce liquid until syrupy. Set aside.

4. Prepare fire for direct-heat method (see page 6). When fire is ready, place melon slices in a grilling basket and lightly grill until lightly browned.

5. To serve, pour reserved syrup over melons, season melons with a grinding of white pepper and a squeeze of lemon juice. Garnish with remaining crystallized ginger.

Makes approximately 16 slices.

Index

Note: Page numbers in italics refer to photos

Anchovy Butter 38
Armenian Shish Kabob *44*, 45–46

Beef
    Beijing Barbecue *32*, 33
    Bourbon Tenderloin 28, *29*
    Grilled Steak in Herb Crust *22*, 23
    Santa Maria Barbecue 30, *31*
    Sesame Ribs 24, *25*
    Southwestern Steak Ranchero *26*, 27
    When Is Meat Done? 27
Beijing Barbecue *32*, 33
Bourbon Beef Tenderloin 28, *29*
Burgers, Garden 87
Butterflied Leg o'Lamb 48–49, *49*
Butters, flavored
    Anchovy 38
    Chile-Lime 80
    Cilantro 74, *75*
    Green Onion-Dill 71
    Mustard 69

Chicken Satay 52, *53*
Chile-Lime Butter 80
Chinese Barbecued Pork Loin 42
Cilantro Butter 74, *75*
Cilantro-Turkey Fillets *60*, 61
Cooking Methods 6
Creole Kabobs *68*, 69
Cucumber-Mint Sauce 48–49, *49*

Dilled Salmon Steaks *12*, 71
Dry Spice Rubs 16–17

Fire, the 10–11
Fish and shellfish
    Creole Kabobs *68*, 69
    Dilled Salmon Steaks *12*, 71
    Grilled Fish Diablo *72*, 73
    Grilled Lemon-Pepper Clams 70
    Grilled Lobster with Garden Vinaigrette *62*, 63
    Grilling Times for Fish 65
    Mesquite-Grilled Swordfish 74, *75*

Mexican-Style Shrimp Skewers 66, *67*
Oysters Mignonette 64, *65*
Tips for Grilling Fish 71
Flavoring the Fire 57
Fruit
    Gingered Grilled Melon 94
    Grilled Kabobs 92, *93*
    Jamaican Banana Grill *88*, 89
    Pineapple-Citrus Skewers 90
    Tips for Grilling Fruit 91
Fuels and Firestarters 8–11

Garden Burgers 87
Garden Vinaigrette 63
Georgia Chicken *50*, 51
Georgia Sauce *18*, 19
Gingered Grilled Melon 94
Green Onion-Dill Butter 71
Grilled Breast of Duck 58, *59*
Grilled Fish Diablo *72*, 73
Grilled Fruit Kabobs 92, *93*
Grilled Japanese Eggplant 79
Grilled Lemon-Pepper Clams 70
Grilled Lobster with Garden Vinaigrette *62*, 63
Grilled Polenta *82*, 83
Grilled Rock Cornish Game Hens 57
Grilled Steak in Herb Crust *22*, 23
Grilled Vegetable Fajitas 78
Grilling Times for Fish 65
Grills, types of 6–8

Herbal Skewers 53

Jamaican Banana Grill *88*, 89

Kabobs
    Armenian Shish Kabob *44*, 45–46
    Chicken Satay 52, *53*
    Creole *68*, 69
    Grilled Fruit 92, *93*
    Grilled Vegetable Fajitas 78
    Herbal Skewers 53
    Mexican-Style Shrimp Skewers 66, *67*
    Pineapple-Citrus Skewers 90
    Sicilian Spiedini 38
    Timing Grilled Skewers 66
Kansas City Sauce 21
Kids Cooking at the Grill 86

Lamb
    Armenian Shish Kabob *44*, 45–46
    Butterflied Leg o'Lamb 48–49, *49*
    Spicy Lamb Chop Grill *46*, 47
Lemon-Basted Chicken 56, *85*
Lemon-Pepper Vinegar 70

Marinades and spice rubs
    Mustard and Herb *14*, 15
    Spice Rub for Fish 17
    Spice Rub for Meat 16, *17*
    Spice Rub for Poultry 16
    Teriyaki *14*, 15
Mesquite-Grilled Swordfish 74, *75*
Mexican-Style Shrimp Skewers 66,
    67
Microwave-Boosted Barbecue 43
Mignonette Sauce 64
Mustard and Herb Marinade *14*, 15
Mustard Butter 69

North Carolina Sauce 19

Old-Fashioned Barbecued Pork Ribs
    34, 35
Oysters Mignonette 64, *65*

Pineapple-Citrus Skewers 90
Pollo Pequeño *54*, 55
Pork
    Adobo *40*, 41
    Chinese Barbecued Loin 42
    Chops Dijon 39, *39*
    Old-Fashioned Barbecued Ribs
    34, 35
    Sicilian Spiedini 38
    Thai Barbecued Ribs 36, *37*
Pork Adobo *40*, 41
Pork Chops Dijon 39, *39*
Poultry
    Chicken Satay 52, *53*
    Cilantro-Turkey Fillets *60*, 61
    Georgia Chicken *50*, 51
    Grilled Breast of Duck 58, *59*
    Grilled Rock Cornish Game
      Hens 57
    Lemon-Basted Chicken 56, *85*
    Pollo Pequeño *54*, 55
    Safety Tips for Fresh Poultry 61
    When Is Poultry Done? 55
Preparing Eggplant for the Grill 79
Preparing the Grill 7

Roasted Garlic 86
Roasted Red Peppers 84, *85*

Safety Tips 11
Safety Tips for Fresh Poultry 61
Salsa Cruda 31
Santa Maria Barbecue 30, *31*
Sauces
    Cucumber-Mint 48–49, *49*
    Garden Vinaigrette 63
    Georgia *18*, 19
    Kansas City 21
    Mignonette 64
    North Carolina 19
    Salsa Cruda 31
    Sour Cream 92, *93*
    Texas 20, *20*
    Thai Dipping 36, *37*
Sesame Beef Ribs 24, *25*
Sicilian Spiedini 38
Sour Cream Sauce 92, *93*
Southwestern Steak Ranchero 26,
    27
Spicy Lamb Chop Grill *46*, 47
Sweet Corn with Chile-Lime Butter
    80, *81*

Teriyaki Marinade *14*, 15
Texas Sauce 20, *20*
Thai Barbecued Ribs 36, *37*
Thai Dipping Sauce 36, *37*
Timing Grilled Skewers 66
Tips for Grilling Fish 71
Tips for Grilling Fruit 91

Vegetable Mixed Grill *76*, 77
Vegetables
    Garden Burgers 87
    Grilled Japanese Eggplant 79
    Grilled Polenta *82*, 83
    Grilled Vegetable Fajitas 78
    Preparing Eggplant for the Grill
      79
    Roasted Garlic 86
    Roasted Red Peppers 84, *85*
    Sweet Corn with Chile-Lime
      Butter 80, *81*
    Vegetable Mixed Grill *76*, 77

When Is Meat Done? 27
When Is Poultry Done? 55